Other Books by Robert Townsend

Up the Organization
Further Up the Organization

THE B² CHRONICLES

HOW NOT TO BUTT HEADS WITH THE NEXT GENERATION

ROBERT TOWNSEND

Pfeiffer & COMPANY

Amsterdam • Johannesburg • Oxford
San Diego • Sydney • Toronto

Copyright © 1994 by Pfeiffer & Company

8517 Production Avenue
San Diego, CA 92121-2280

This publication is designed to provide accurate and authoritative information in regard to the subject matter covered. It is sold with the understanding that the publisher is not engaged in rendering legal, accounting, or other professional service. If legal advice or other expert assistance is required, the services of a competent professional person should be sought. *From a Declaration of Principles jointly adopted by a Committee of the American Bar Association and a Committee of Publishers.*

Cover design concept: Rick de Lome
Cover design production: Frank Schiele
Cover photograph: © W. Warren/West Light
Photograph on page 21: Mary Stewart Cook
All other photography and interior design: Jeffrey Townsend

Editor: JoAnn Padgett
Project Coordinator: Kathleen Deming
Assistant Editor: Heidi Erika Callinan

Library of Congress Cataloging-in-Publication Data
Townsend, Robert, 1920-
    The B² chronicles, or, How not to butt heads with the next generation / Robert Townsend.
    p.   cm.
    ISBN 0-89384-266-4
      1. Management. 2. Organization. 3. Social groups. I. Title.
    II. Title: How not to butt heads with the next generation.
    HD31.T668 1994
    650.1—dc20   94-19874
                                               CIP

Printed in the United States of America.
Printing 1 2 3 4 5 6 7 8 9 10

To Saint Joan

Acknowledgments

The author would like to thank Kathleen Deming, Karla Swatek and Jeffrey Townsend for virtually organizing him and making the project fun. He invites them to participate if B^2 becomes a TV cartoon series.

This is a sequel to *Up the Organization*. Having started by trying to help the establishment in 1970, I'd like to begin this time from the other end, by seeing what we can do for our youth: let's call them the Beavis and Butt-Head Generation, or B^2 for short.

Some people might ask: "Why help Beavis and Butt-Head? Why not let nature take its course and let the appalling outcome develop? After all, most of their teachers and coaches have given up on them, haven't they? And their parents are joyfully blowing the college money on cars, condos, and trips to Cancun, aren't they?"

Hey, the B^2 Generation is going to survive just like we survived. And don't tell me you were never Beavis or Butt-Head because I know better. I was. Everybody I know was. Some of us evolved sooner and some evolved better because we got help from some unexpected sources.

Me, I got helped by WWII. *[That's World War Two, Butt-Head.]* It was a good war against evil enemies; it brought a lot of people and equipment together in a grand, chaotic, sometimes exciting, sometimes boring mass effort to win. And win we did, probably because we were eight times as rich and only twice as stupid as the evil enemies.

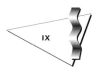

It's time some unexpected source laid some help on the B^2 Generation, and the only way I can get involved is to write to you Geezers and Boomers—B^2 people don't read much beyond comic books, TV listings, and computer screens. In *Up the Organization*, I tried to tell you straight out what worked for me, what didn't work, what I thought you should try, and what you might try to avoid. This effort is more indirect. I'm trying to amuse and entertain you a little while occasionally slipping a useful thought under the door. Maybe as you read, you'll stumble over some ideas that might help you and others who will give B2 their first enjoyable work.

RT
April 3, 1994
Reno, Nevada

Each noble action
is selfish. Saving them I
also save myself.

Introduction

I am not at all sure where I found the disk containing The B^2 Chronicles. It was probably the Bennis-O'Toole Wing of the QuoVadoTron DEpot in San Pedro. That's where I was doing most of my research in the year 2040, which was certainly the year I found the disk.

DEpots were the free, 24-hour, self-service Disk Exchange Centers that operated on the honor system (take two, leave two). They came about after the old county and city libraries had become moribund.

My research reveals that back in the bad old days, before QuoVadoTron, organizations often grew larger than 250 people. There are wild stories about organizations with hundreds of thousands of workers. This trend seems to have climaxed in the 1980's, when a few giant organizations began to break themselves up into small, autonomous units in search of the energy that had long since vanished from their offices and plants. In any case, it is clear that most people hated their work and put as little effort into it as they thought they could get away with, saving all of their energy and creativity for evenings, weekends, holidays, and vacations. The world is so different now it's hard to imagine how it used to be.

The B^2 Chronicles is a journal that was kept by a man named Crunch, who, together with my grandfather, Dooley Stepnowski, gave the world QuoVadoTron in 1995. The journal gives us a picture of life as it was soon after QuoVadoTron was invented and before the First and Last World Presidency (FALWP) in 2008. The B^2 Chronicles was written in a ten-month period from 1998 to 1999.

Crunch had evidently been searching for a good way to repay society for some of his QuoVadoTron earnings. He persuaded Dooley and Archibald—two other refugees from mega-companies—to join him in helping the struggling new generation, which was then called "B^2" after a couple of reprehensible cartoon kids named Beavis and Butt-Head.

Most of you are probably already familiar with the headline stories about the First and Last World Presidency and the speculation about why the two major world powers suddenly shook hands in 2008 and broke up into collections of tiny organizations. Crunch's last entry in the Chronicles, dated Christmas Day of that year, was a file named simply "READ ME FIRST." It explains for the first time the mysterious background events that led to...Oh, why not let Crunch tell the story?

Jennifer Stepnowski
San Pedro, California
August 2065

Every age and generation must be as free to act for itself, in all cases, as the age and generation which preceded it.... Man has no property in man; neither has any generation a property in the generations which are to follow.

Thomas Paine, *The Rights of Man*

READ ME FIRST

I was reading the paper one morning in the spring of 2008, and saw that the world had been brought to a state of acute anxiety by a report issued by the Institute for International and Strategic Studies in London.

Based on a leak from the British intelligence unit M.I.5, the report gave the following humdrum data on nuclear disarmament: all the missiles in the world had been destroyed except the last 2,400. Russia and America each retained 1,200 weapons to demonstrate their rights as former superpowers to be the last to disarm. These remaining missiles were aimed at targets randomly selected by a computer that had no data on race, religion, creed, or population density.

Then the Institute revealed the startling news that all 2,400 of the remaining weapons were linked to a single, closed circuit designed to fire simultaneously if any effort was made to tamper with them or fail to supply them with their daily diet of fuel and replacement parts.

This strategy, called the Mutual Destruction Scenario (MDS), was conjectured to have been secretly arranged by the military and industrial leaders of Russia and America to protect the privileges that they have enjoyed for the last 50 years.

Military leaders from both nations had second thoughts when they learned that computer hackers had infiltrated the system and planted a virus that would trigger detonation and turn the planet into toast in six months.

"The MDS is imperfect," an anonymous general was quoted as saying. "I have just learned that, under Pentagon rules, if I am dead, I lose my pension."

Buried deep in the report was the revelation that no plan for deactivation of the MDS had yet been devised or could ever be created, at least by theoretical means. An empirical process might work, but, obviously, no one had ever tried it.

Three days later, a fleet of black limousines pulled up at our storefront in San Pedro. A squad of generals and admirals entered, led by two men in charcoal-grey suits, one speaking with a Russian accent.

"Okay, Mr. Crunch," the Russian gentleman said, "We know what you're up to. Two years ago your director of research, one Dooley Stepnowski, developed a game, the so-called Nuclear Lemmings, yes? The design and interface of this game bears, shall we say, a certain resemblance to our top-secret program, MDS. Do you follow what I am saying?"

The American took over, impatient. "Look. Our information tells us that out of the 641,812 times the program was played here in the last nine years, the missiles in the game were deactivated 21 times by players using 17 different code names."

The American leaned closer. "I'm not going to beat around the bush, my friend. We want the names of those 17 kids."

I cleared my throat. I'll admit, I was milking the moment.

"Archibald told us to expect you," I told them. "We'll give you the names."

"Very good," said the American.

"You see? Democracy in action," chuckled the Russian gentleman.

"That's exactly right," I said, as I reached into one of the file cabinets and pulled out a rolled document and untied the ribbon around it. Archibald always loved a traditional flourish.

They looked at the document, and then at me. I smiled.

"These are our terms."

Terms to Save the World

Preamble

The last time of universal peace was the Pax Romana. The power of Rome was based on its legions. The power of the legions was based on the centurions, who led 100 men and knew each of them intimately. Units of people have been growing in size ever since, and the world has been going from worse to impossible.

Now, therefore, the Congress of People's Deputies of Russia and the Congress of the United States, in a joint session presided over by their respective presidents,

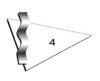

Agree

1. That both presidents will forthwith resign;

2. That Juanita-Maria Francesca of San Pedro, California, will immediately be elected to succeed them both and be designated as The World's First and Last President;

3. That the new president's only act in office will be to sign a prepackaged amendment to the constitutions of the United States and Russia, providing that no business, university, club, union, or other institution may ever consist of more than 250 people and that no government unit may ever be larger than the city of San Pedro, California.

4. That the new president will thereupon surrender the names of the 17 kids who can deactivate MDS, and resign immediately thereafter.

Dooley, Juanita-Maria, and I drove to the airport to get our standby seats on Wild West Airlines to the Presidential Inauguration/Resignation ceremonies in Washington. I was eager to get back the next day because I wanted to go fishing. The albacore were feeding north of Catalina.

"Do you suppose that other little burgs the size of San Pedro will pick up on our storefronts?" asked Stepnowski.

"That's up to them," I said.

One certainty: no
matter how many fresh starts,
we'll always spoil it.

THE STOREFRONT

My name is Crunch.

I took my share of the daily royalty check from QuoVadoTron and rented a storefront in San Pedro.

It had a big room in front, an office in the back, and an apartment upstairs. My plan was to create a test center with the newest experimental virtual reality games and to let kids play free if they earned membership cards as volunteer test pilots by keeping their grades up in school.

Enough manufacturers signed up to fill the big front room with games, and I had a feeling the rest would fall in line soon.

Dooley Stepnowski—the world's greatest self-employed computer programmer, electronic repairman and supercool game wizard—quickly signed on to keep the games running and to create some new games in return for the apartment upstairs and a continuous supply of fresh grapefruit, Philly FREE, Kozlowski Farms Apple Butter, whole-wheat pita, red leaf lettuce, oatmeal, pinto beans, brown rice, Colombian coffee beans, and nonfat milk powder. All tools and supplies were to be delivered promptly on request.

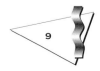

9

The test center was open from 3 p.m. to 6 p.m. I put a sign in the window:

> Volunteer video game test pilots needed.
> Apply here between 3 p.m. and 6 p.m.

When the kids drifted in and spied the array of machines, the first thing they were told was that they had to fill out an application.

It needn't be cool
as long as it doesn't suck.
That's most important.

TEST PILOT APPLICATION

Name _____

Birthdate _____ Age _____

Address _____

_____

Telephone _____

Mother lives where? _____

Father lives where? _____

Name of your school _____

Grade _____

Homeroom Teacher _____

13

Do you like video games?_____

If you are accepted as a test pilot, will you be able to get your homework done and keep your grades above passing? _____

I agree to bring a copy of each report card to the test center on the day I get it.

Signed _____

Fun sometimes leads to
opportunities to win.
A matter of luck.

REPORT CARDS

After the test center was humming smoothly, the first report cards were handed over to Dooley, who logged them into our mainframe. Each month he printed out three lists: those who improved or stayed the same, those who got worse but still passed, and those who failed or didn't turn in report cards.

These lists were kept confidential. Nothing was said about report cards. Everyone who was passing got a new 30-day ID card; the others didn't. Dooley modified the CPUs so that they could only be turned on by valid ID cards; stragglers automatically lost access to the games.

In most cases this encouraged a positive response, and many early slackers became average or top students and regained their test pilot credentials. Only a few dropped out of the program.

The big bell curve of
life: a few great, a few poor;
then the rest of us.

I Hire a Lawyer

It was clear to me from the start of this project that the only people who wouldn't be angry and obstructive would be the kids who were using the games and the people who hadn't heard about it yet.

My initial list of probable opponents included parents, teachers, school administrators, politicians, government officials, police, press, and assorted busybodies.

So before I rented the storefront, I telephoned the world's greatest lawyer and negotiator, Archibald Petrie. He lives in Wainscott, Suffolk County, Long Island, New York, in the midst of sand dunes and potato farms. He picked that location because it was near Seymour, the best elevator repairman in the eastern half of the country. Archibald, with his bad back, needs an elevator, and the elevator needs a repairman.

Archibald and I have been partners in various ventures in the past, all of them fun. Before we met, each of us had discovered a strong connection between fun and success. We always worked on the same basis: He got half of whatever I got and worked no more than half-time. So when I offered him the opportunity to become general counsel to the

19

test center, I pointed out that he could either work for half of nothing or pay half my expenses and work for nothing. He chose the former.

In addition to being the world's greatest lawyer and negotiator, Archibald has the names and telephone numbers of the 300,000 people in the world who make things happen and know how to get things done in federal, state, and municipal government; in corporations; associations; news media; and in law firms. Twelve large yellow phone directories with these names and phone numbers crowd the surface of his desk. If anybody anywhere tried to make trouble for my project, I knew I could call Archibald, he would look in a yellow directory, make a phone call, and soon the trouble would go away. Not by menace or threat, you understand, but by means of a lucid explanation of the facts and pertinent ramifications.

So the test center had some protection by the wise and well-connected against the forces of ignorance.

Trying something new
is bad enough. Doing good:
the final insult.

WHO AM I?

As I said, my name is Crunch. I've asked Dooley to fill you in. Before he does, I've got to define a couple of terms that are going to keep popping up: "Fetchwork" and "Stretchwork." When we were building QuoVadoTron, Dooley and I made up these words to measure energy expenditure in the workplace.

In a nutshell, Fetchwork 0 is the kind of energy your son displays when you yell at him to get out of bed and go mow the lawn. Stretchwork 10 describes the energy you'd display if your wife said "Jack Nicklaus is calling from the club; he wants you right away to make a fourth."

There are twenty degrees of measurement in between.

Here's Dooley.

Facilitator
for folks who would change their lives
from Fetch- to Stretch-work.

CRUNCH BY DOOLEY

Crunch is an O.K. geezer. We've known each other for a long time, even worked in different parts of a big company once. He's essentially lazy, mildly bad-tempered, and addicted to no-brainer mystery fiction. He claims he only reads writers who are underappreciated outside their own genre, like Lawrence Block, Robert Campbell, Amanda Cross, Jonathan Gash, Martha Grimes, Carl Hiassen, Reginald Hill, Tony Hillerman, Elmore Leonard, and Ross Thomas.

His standout feature is an off-the-wall mind that continuously feeds him unusual takes on whatever he's thinking about. That makes him a good partner when you're trying to create something, like when we came up with a software program for small companies called QuoVadoTron, which made us some serious money. But Crunch can sure make it painful when you interrupt him in his reading room.

It isn't a reading room, actually; that's just what he calls it. It's the whole roof of the storefront. There's a beautiful view of San Pedro harbor when the fog has burned off. The roof is flat and empty except for the structure that contains the air conditioning unit, the telephone stuff, and some electrical equipment. Crunch has added a waterproof* lean-to, which holds his chair, folding table, a small refrigerator, and a half-dozen gallons of distilled water. A 100-foot orange power cord from the office down below supplies the power for the fridge and for his coffee maker, which he takes downstairs and washes before he leaves every evening so that it will be clean the next morning.

This gives you a picture of the way Crunch thinks. Me, I'd know there was water and power on the roof, and I'd tap those and wash the coffee maker on the roof and dispense with the long, orange power cord.

Anyway, that's Crunch and he's a good guy.

*You might think we wouldn't need waterproofing in San Pedro, but you'd be wrong. The marine layer gives us a wetting every morning and evening, except when the Santa Ana winds are blowing out of the north.

Dooley left out a
lot of favorite writers:
wordsmiths with humor.

QuoVadoTron

It's time you knew more about QuoVadoTron.

Some years before the storefront project in San Pedro, Dooley and I were working for a big company that is better left unnamed.

One night I got an inspiration, and the next day I asked Dooley to join me for a drink after work.

"Dooley," I said, "I don't think this company will ever be a good place to work. It's too big. But I've got the germ of an idea to help smaller companies hang on to their energy."

"Cut to the chase, Crunch," said Dooley. "I'm not getting any younger."

"Okay. We know the big companies are downsizing and that for years they haven't been good places to work. So let's think about the companies with between 250 and 1,000 employees, where it's still fun to work. Most of them know about the dangers of getting big. Let's give them some software to help them keep their work exciting."

Dooley raised an eyebrow. "What do you have in mind, Crunch?"

"Take a company of about 250 people. Call it Droids R Us. They lease our software. Call it Energy Compass or something. They rent a high school auditorium for a Friday afternoon, a Saturday, and a Sunday, equip it with your basic balloting booths outfitted with computers, and at 2 p.m. Friday, they call an all-hands meeting in the auditorium.

"'Here's what we're gonna do,' they say. 'We want to find out what everybody thinks about how they're doing, how the whole company's doing, and how the boss is doing.

"'And to make sure the data is not misused, we're going to prevent anybody from seeing anything except the following:

1. **What is the company goal?**
2. **What is the XYZ department (or division) goal?**
3. **How is the XYZ department (or division) allocating its energy?**
4. **How am I personally allocating my energy?**
5. **How do I think the boss is allocating energy?**
6. **How is the boss actually allocating energy?**

"'To get all that information out, we all have to put information in. Here's what we're asking you to do this weekend:

"'Rate all the people you work with on a scale of 0 (low) to 10 (high) in four categories.

1. **Character**
2. **Energy**
3. **Knowledge of the business**
4. **Focus on company (or department/division) goal**

"'Then answer 12 questions.

1. **What is the goal of the company?**
2. **What is the goal of your department or division?**
3. **How is your department or division doing? (0 to 10)**
4. **How is the whole company doing? (0 to 10)**
5. **Is there one major problem affecting you? If so, who or what is it?**
6. **What is the relative justice of pay in the company? (0 to 10)**
7. **Name the unneeded departments/divisions in the company.**
8. **What excuses do you personally have for not being your best?**
9. **How much "them and us" conflict is there? (0 to 10)**
10. **How many signatures do you have to get to do or buy something?**
11. **How much fun is it working here? (0 to 10)**
12. **Anything else? Describe it.**

31

"'We'll take all of the data and generate reports to show everybody how the company thinks it's doing.'"

"Piece of cake," said Dooley. "Call it QuoVadoTron, or QVT for short."

"Whatever. Now here's the critical part," I told him. "I'm convinced there are lots of different energy levels at work in a company at any given time. Let me give you a couple of examples.

"Ted, a vice president, is a thoroughly despicable upward fawner and downward slave driver. He knows that another v.p., Jack, is on vacation. He goes to Jack's secretary, Nora, and gives her some typing to do. This is Fetchwork, and will get the lowest level of energy possible. Let's call this level Fetchwork 0 or FW-0.

"At the other extreme, your boss, whom you admire and respect, comes to you, explains an exciting new project she's going to be heading, asks you to drop everything and come work with her on it. That's probably the highest level of energy you are capable of—Stretchwork 10 or SW-10. And in between FW-0 and SW-10 there are twenty other levels.

"I want to help small companies measure their various energies. Can you set it up so people can discover the level of energy they apply to all their activities?"

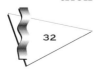

"Yeah, I think so," said Dooley. "Can you describe what you want the program to produce, exactly?"

"Well, I think QuoVadoTron should print out a diagram, sort of like a compass, that shows, visually, where and how much energy is being expended, in a company at any level. The data I think people should be able to access would have to include the following:

1. Company goal
2. How people are spending their energy, companywide
3. Average energy level, in the company, FW-0 to SW-10
4. Our department/division goal
5. Average energy level in my department/division, FW-0 to SW-10
6. How the boss is actually allocating his energy
7. Boss's perceived energy allocation
8. Personal allocation of energy within my department/division
9. Personal average energy level per activity, FW-0 to SW-10

"All of that can be done, Crunch, but will anybody use it?"

"Dooley," I said, "if all the people at Droids R Us can be persuaded that they won't be zapped by this program, and if they believe that it's more fun if everyone knows what the goal is, agrees on it, and works at SW-5 instead of FW-5, then that's going to be one great place to work.

And their big competitor, Cyborg City, is going to have to find out how Droids R Us is doing it or go out of business."

So Dooley created the program, we picked a company to try it out on, and with their enthusiastic help, we began to tweak it into shape.

First to go was my image of the high school auditorium. Dooley reminded me that this could all be done with a secure e-mail system, and nobody had to leave their desks. I guess I just liked the idea of those musty voting booths. I got over it eventually.

But it made me think. All the lecturers on organization, management, and leadership must be wondering why they've had so little impact in the last ten years.

They should have imagined themselves in the position of their target, the boss.

We were all after the big ones. Think of Roger Smith of General Motors, for example. There he was, just got the job, listening to all of us twits telling him to change it all.

He just realized his wildest dream, and you want him to change it and the system that got him there? *"To the moon, Alice!"*

Even if you did get some attention from the business schools and some of the more adventurous companies and GM's board of directors got interested as a result, where's the motivation for Roger?

He'll form a committee to study what kind of a task force should be appointed to hire which consultants to start a study of how to apply your ideas to GM. *"Come on, Alice, get real!"*

We've got to target the bosses who really want their companies to stay exciting, and the hook is FUN. We've got to make it as easy and as much fun as possible for them and their people because we all know that change is PAIN.

So let's create great software and teach the bosses who need it, know they need it, and want it, how to use it. As they test it out, learn from them, improve it, fix it, and make it FUN. And let's hope the next ten years aren't as misguided as the last ten.

Well, that's all you need to know about QuoVadoTron. What you've got here, including the next chapter and the notes on the energy compasses, will give you a better feel than a six-month contract with a QVT facilitator, which would cost you megabucks. Anyway, QVT is history. Its only relevance here is that it is paying for the San Pedro storefront experiments.

Energy and fun:
those are the keys to success.
Get that right—you win!

How QuoVadoTron Works

QuoVadoTron (QVT) is a reality check.

By putting the CEO's diaries and telephone logs on real time, it gives a continuous reading of the directions in which the boss's energies are spent. By analyzing the weekly inputs of all the employees, it also measures (among many other things) how the CEO's energy is perceived to be spent.

Gaps between these readings indicate confusion at best.

It also continuously delivers the perceived goal of the company (and of each division and department) and will, upon request, tell individuals how they are allocating their energy.

A fish and an organization rot from the head down. If the chief is working hard and smart toward a generally understood and accepted company goal, that's O.K., and we're O.K. If not, not.

As you can imagine, QVT only works if the boss wants everybody to know the truth about everything.

Of course, that's not all QVT does, or I wouldn't have gotten so wealthy inventing it with Dooley.

We designed the software for companies whose CEOs sincerely want to keep the energy level high and let everybody know where they're going.*

*Not necessarily to see God, which was where Jesus said he was going when he complained (Vulgate Bible, St. John 16.5) that none of his disciples had asked Him: "Quo Vadis?" or "Whither goest thou?" This was what Dooley was thinking about when he named our product QuoVadoTron.

Depends on the boss;
truth and justice seekers all
attract Stretch-workers.

QuoVadoTron Energy Compass Template

COORDINATES:
COMPANY:
NO. OF EMPLOYEES:
CEO:
AGE:
AVERAGE ENERGY
** LEVEL—COMPANY**
** GOAL: SW-2**
QUERY:

Goal of Company

Community Work

Entertainment

Professional Organizations

Trade Organizations

Customer Feedback

Customer Service

Participation Sports

Spectator Sports

Conferences

Seminars

Unnecessary Memos

Charitable Organizations

Consultants

Product Design

Manufacturing

Unnecessary Meetings

Board of Directors

Ego Trips & Junkets

Marketing

Sales

Outside Directorships

The chart on the facing page is a template of the energy compass and the input prompts employees will respond to.

The prompts around the compass will vary from company to company and for each division, department, and individual.

Inputs are made weekly by e-mail and range from the mandatory minimum to whatever it takes for the individual to flag the problem.

As for access, Dooley and I always favored openness; secrecy is overrated as an asset and underrated as a liability. Clients vary. Generally, the more successful they are, the more open they are.

I don't want to make this a QVT operating manual. Suffice it to say that the genius of QVT comes from its combination of "hard" and "soft" data manipulation. In calculating "average energy levels," for example, it is quite remarkable in its ability to identify and reject "sports" or misleading inputs. At the other extreme, it is very sensitive to word usage and evaluates Freudian slips with interesting accuracy. It is hard to fool QVT. Dooley and I deserve less credit for this than we get; we piggybacked on the years of artificial intelligence work that preceded QVT.

Most clients respect and trust the "average energy level" estimates and they enjoy the ability to watch the effect of organizational changes on a daily basis, although we keep insisting that weekly readings are far more reliable.

COORDINATES: CEO
COMPANY: Droids R Us
NO. OF EMPLOYEES: 250
CEO: Sterling Mentor
AGE: 45
AVERAGE ENERGY
  LEVEL—COMPANY
  GOAL: SW-6
QUERY: How is CEO
  actually
  allocating
  his energy?

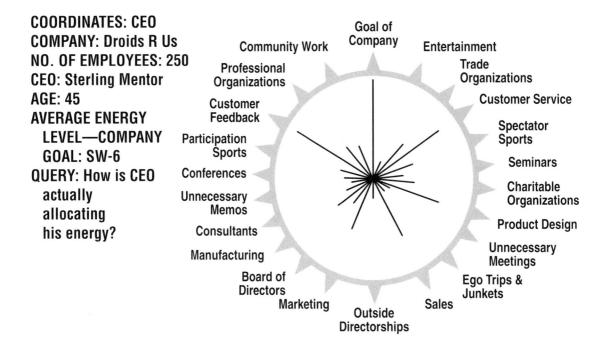

EVALUATION: This is typical of a healthy, energetic company.

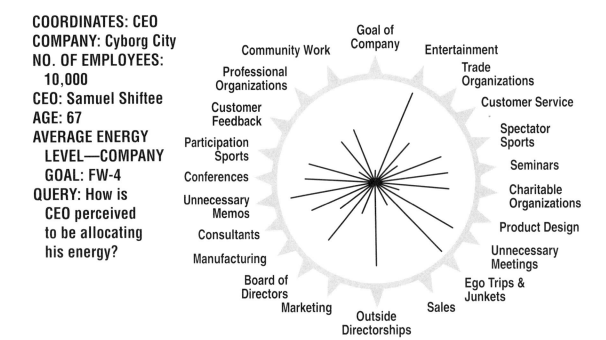

COORDINATES: CEO
COMPANY: Cyborg City
NO. OF EMPLOYEES:
   10,000
CEO: Samuel Shiftee
AGE: 67
AVERAGE ENERGY
   LEVEL—COMPANY
   GOAL: FW-4
QUERY: How is
   CEO perceived
   to be allocating
   his energy?

Goal of Company

Community Work

Entertainment

Professional Organizations

Trade Organizations

Customer Feedback

Customer Service

Participation Sports

Spectator Sports

Conferences

Seminars

Unnecessary Memos

Charitable Organizations

Consultants

Product Design

Manufacturing

Unnecessary Meetings

Board of Directors

Ego Trips & Junkets

Marketing

Sales

Outside Directorships

44

EVALUATION: This is typical of a company about to terminate its QVT contract. Access by employees has been severely restricted. Although Mr. Shiftee's interest in the company goal seems minimal, he will undoubtedly be working at SW-8 when it comes to saving his own job. No CEO has ever been found less than wise, determined, creative, and decisive in the pursuit of personal security.

DOOLEY'S STOREFRONT LABORATORY

Dooley came to me one day with an idea for a game called Klass Klown. After he described it to me, I asked what he needed to create it.

"Some space and some equipment for a dust-free lab to create new games," he said. So that's how we got the storefront next door.

Dooley needed an assistant to help set up his lab, so we posted a notice in the window:

> Assistant Video Game Designer Needed

Too many kids applied because everybody loved Dooley and wanted to work with him. We devised a contest; the winner would become Dooley's assistant.

Space, time, money are
important; inspiration
is the catalyst.

THE CONTEST

The rules of the contest to decide who would be Dooley's assistant were to go to an Army, Navy, Marine, or Air Force recruiting station and come back with all the information that was important, such as the following:

> *How do you join?*
>
> *What education requirement is there? How old do you have to be?*
>
> *Once in, how much choice do you have about:*
>
> > *Where you go? What kind of training you get?*
>
> *How much do you get paid? How long is a tour of duty?*
>
> *How early can you retire? What is the current pension for early retirees?*
>
> *What would prevent the service from accepting you?*
>
> > *Disease? Conviction of certain crimes?*
>
> *Anything else you think is important.*

As the kids ran out like the Baker Street Irregulars, it occurred to me that we could now add the military as potential opponents of our project.

49

Thinking isn't hard.
It's fun when you get to choose
what to think about.

THE WINNER

The winner was Jeffrey Tours, a young man with an extraordinary memory and fine organizational abilities. His oral report on his visit to a recruiting station was masterful.

"Okay, here goes: to join you gotta be 17; you gotta get a parent's signature; you gotta have a high school diploma; you can't have any felony charges or any unpaid, you know, tickets or law violations; you gotta pass a full physical; and you gotta pass this aptitude test-thing, known as ASVAB *[Armed Services Vocational Aptitude Battery, Beavis].*

"The guy at the Army Recruiting Station, Sergeant Alan Stagg, told me that if I get through a four-year enlistment, they'll give me twenty-five thousand bucks to spend on college.

"He said that to get into electronics I have to do good on the math in the aptitude test, but that's no sweat. They'll train me in electronics and, get this, they'll pay me while I'm learning! I can get out at age 37 with a pension of like a thousand bucks a month, with total health benefits for life for me and Kristie and the tadpoles if, you know, we ever get married and breed, and I could spend all my time working on video games like Dooley!"

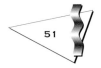

51

He paused to catch his breath. He looked at us suspiciously. "Does anybody else know about this?"

We can do worse than start life at thirty-seven with a nice pension.

KLASS KLOWN

The game Dooley created with Jeffrey Tours could do what the self-appointed comedian in any classroom in America will tend to do: write humorous lyrics to the melodies of popular songs. All you had to tell the computer was

Type of dance, music, or song: Ballad, waltz, rumba, rock, blues, tango, salsa, bossa nova, reggae, calypso, march, sea chantey, etc.
Feeling: Love, hate, jealousy, anger, fear, joy, ecstasy, humor, revenge, sorrow, misgiving.
Story: What's the song about?

Dooley let me request the first lyric, so I typed the following

Blues
Sorrow
A child is walking with her father. Her friends see her and laugh at her. She is embarrassed.

The computer waited a moment and then generated the title:

'Shamed of Daddy Blues

Singing, poetry,
and humor are as old as
cave drawings in France.

'SHAMED OF DADDY BLUES

I've got the red hot 'Shamed of Daddy Blues.
I've got the red hot 'Shamed of Daddy Blues.
I walk on the other side of the street,
Pretend I belong to someone neat.

I've got the red hot 'Shamed of Daddy Blues.
I've got the red hot 'Shamed of Daddy Blues.
I see as little of him as I can,
I like to pretend he's the handyman.

I've got the red hot 'Shamed of Daddy Blues.
I've got the red hot 'Shamed of Daddy Blues.
He's narrow in the shoulders and broad in the waist,
He's the biggest problem I ever faced.

I've got the red
Hot
'Shamed of Daddy Blues.

If parents could see
through children's eyes, behavior
would alter greatly.

THE MIDNIGHT MISSION

Dooley had come up with another game idea, ThunderBuns, and as usual we were flooded with applicants for the job of assisting him.

Our contest to pick a winner involved going to a mission in downtown Los Angeles that ministered to the homeless and bewildered and to find out all about it, including what was different about it.

The winner was Bud Shrake; he found the Midnight Mission.

This is what he told us:

"See, this Midnight Mission has been around for a million years [*since 1911, Bud*]. They pick up these old geezers living on the street, delouse 'em, shave 'em, give 'em new threads, feed 'em dinner, give 'em a bed for the night and breakfast when they wake up. All the geezers have to do is work three hours a day to keep the joint clean.

"It's a real rainbow. They don't care who you are, what you look like, or what you believe; only thing is, you can't be a woman and stay overnight. They got no whatchamacallit...facilities.

"So I guess there's not much action there at night.

59

"The dude who runs the place is Clancy Imislund who's been there like forever *[since 1974, Bud]*. He makes sure all the *dinero* they take in gets spent on the geezers, which is cool."*

*Bud means they don't advertise; they just send out two mail solicitations a year. He also neglected to report that MM is at 396 South Los Angeles Street (in Los Angeles, California) and serves 44,000 meals (to men and women), provides 5,000 shaves and showers, 4,500 beds and 1,000 articles of clothing each month. Bud's report wouldn't have gotten him on the payroll at *The Washington Post*, but we thought it was pretty good for a kid with his knees sticking out of his jeans and his cap on backwards.

There but for the grace
of God go I and all my
family and friends.

THUNDERBUNS

Dooley Stepnowski was a sort of fitness freak. "Sort of" is an apt modifier because Dooley was no vegan *[that's no meat, no dairy, Beavis]*, just a person who knew he felt better when he felt better and knew what caused him to feel better or worse.

All this to explain Dooley's second game: ThunderBuns. The game had a built-in camera that would photograph you when you started to play. Your face and body appeared from the waist up. You began by watching yourself eating at meal times, snacking between meals, and exercising.

You controlled what and how much you consumed; nutritional labels of what you were eating and drinking appeared in windows on the screen. Time was foreshortened in this game and, as you programmed your meals, snacks, exercise programs, smoking, and alcohol consumption, your appearance changed and you aged as you watched. As your intake of cholesterol, fat, salt, sugar, nicotine, and alcohol was tabulated, the risk factors of diabetes, heart attack, stroke, and cirrhosis flashed on the screen. Blood pressure was monitored continuously.

By changing your eating, drinking, smoking, and exercise habits, you could watch yourself appear to grow younger even though you were still aging chronologically. It was great fun to set a terrible program and then to fast-forward to see what you died of. It was less fun to get back in shape.

After playing the game a few times and watching the labels of all those high-density, refined and processed fat-, sugar-, salt-, and choles-terol-filled products flash on the screen as they were being consumed, I knew we could count on the meat, cheese, processed food, tobacco, and distillery companies as well as the fast-food franchises to be among our most active enemies.

Learning comes through the
door marked "play" more often than
the "study" portal.

YOUNGER MAN

Game: Klass Klown
Type of dance, music, or song: Calypso
Feeling: Boredom
Story: Young woman married to older man, needs younger companion

I got to get me a younger man,
Maybe not so tall maybe not so tan,
Who'll play with me upon the sand.
I definitely need a younger man.

He'll take me to the beach most every day,
And let me windsurf across the bay.
Three sets of tennis and another swim,
And still he be feeling full of vim.

67

I got to get me a younger man,
Maybe not so tall maybe not so tan,
Who'll play with me upon the sand.
I definitely need a younger man.

He'll take me to the disco every night
And dance with me until midnight,
Then he'll take me home and pleasure me,
Until the cock crow one, two, three.

I got to get me a younger man,
Maybe not so tall maybe not so tan,
Who'll play with me upon the sand.
I definitely need a younger man.

It is not age as
much as it is energy
that mars the marriage.

WE RENT THE STOREFRONT ON THE OTHER SIDE

The game room was overcrowded with test pilots, and manufacturers were pressing us to take more units. They were particularly interested in the real-time suggestion system Dooley had added on to each computer so that the kids could send their likes, dislikes, and enhancement ideas directly to the manufacturers by e-mail. So we rented the storefront on the other side, knocked out the wall between, and expanded our game room.

Dooley needed another assistant to help him keep the computers in good repair, so we asked for volunteers and got too many applicants once more.

So, of course, we announced another contest.

Smaller is better,
but sometimes growing too fast
is a lot of fun.

THE LANGUAGE CONTEST

We asked people to learn to say the following in a foreign language:

One two three four five six seven eight nine ten.

How are you? I'm O.K.

What's your name? My name is _____.

Why are you eating that awful stuff? It will make you grow old, fat, and ugly. If you want to see what you will look like, come with me to the test center and play our "ThunderBuns" game.

The winner of this contest, and Dooley's new assistant for computer repair, was a young woman named Juanita-Maria Francesca, who claimed to have a knack for languages. She picked Spanish, maintaining that, despite her obvious Hispanic name, she had no working knowledge of the tongue.

73

We decided to believe her. Also, hers was the only complete entry. It came out like this.

Uno dos tres quatro cinco seis siete ocho nueve diez.

¿Como estas? Stoy bien.

¿Como te llamas? Me llamo Juanita-Maria Francesca.

¿Por que comes eso cochinada? Le hacerte viejo, gordo, y feo. Si quieres ver como vas a aparacer, venga conmigo al centro de examenes y juega nuestro juego "ThunderBuns."

Competence is more
important than whether your
accent is funny.

POTHOLE POLITICS

Game: Klass Klown
Type of dance, music, or song: Sea Chantey
Feeling: Frustration
Story: Man complains about potholes causing damage to his
    automobile

Fill up the potholes,
Don't break my car in two.
Fill up the potholes,
Don't break my car in two.

With all the talk of high unemployment,
How can the gov'ment take such enjoyment
Watchin' the potholes
Break up my car in two?

The gov'ment tell me
They got no money.
I tell the gov'ment
Don't you be funny.
Fill up the potholes,
Don' break my car in two.

I tell the gov'ment
They got a new role:
Every week each man
Fill up one pothole—
Soon there'll be nothing
To break up my car in two.

Taxes get paid but
expectation of service
is never fulfilled.

DOOLEY INVENTS ANOTHER GAME

Once ThunderBuns was working smoothly and the kids were having a great time killing themselves by eating Twinkies, french fries, and pizza and blowing up like Macy's Day parade figures, and as soon as Juanita-Maria had become an ace mechanic for the computers, Dooley thought up a new game. He said it would be called BadaBing BadaBoom; however, before he could start on it, he'd need another assistant.

So we had to think up another contest.

There's no limit to
what you can do if you don't
care who gets credit.

THE HOMELESS CONTEST

The instructions for this contest were as follows: go to a wilderness outfitting or Army-Navy store and make up a list of survival gear, all of which could be put in a backpack and carried by one young person. Then go home and, after homework and dinner and before TV, assemble as much of the gear as you can find around the house. With your parents' permission, spend the night in the yard or in the garage (but not in the car) or out away from home, if you dare. Finally, they were asked to bring their list of assembled survival gear and to report their night's experience.

The winner of the contest was Floyd Turner, son of a San Pedro commercial fisherman. Floyd assembled the following stuff with his father's help:

Pocket compass
Flashlight, extra batteries
Pocket AM radio, extra batteries
6 oz. bottle of water
Toilet paper

83

Wash cloth, towel
Toothbrush, toothpaste
Comb
Soap
Matches in a watertight canister
Waterproof ground sheet
Lightweight sleeping bag
Blanket
Waterproof poncho
Watch cap
Pocket knife with usual tools
Fishing line, sinkers, hooks
Two Snickers bars

He spent the night on a fuel dock next to a 72-year-old fishing boat named Sea Rose. His reaction after his overnight experience: "I never knew how much stuff I used. Most of the junk I brought I didn't use, and most of what I wanted I didn't have. But it was cool."

Hard to imagine
living without all our things,
which really own us.

BADABING BADABOOM

Dooley's latest program was an ambitious effort. He wanted to create a game that could finish a story if the player just listed plot, characters, and other elements such as time, place, and genre.

Right at the point where most storytellers get flustered and start saying things like "yatta yatta yatta" and "bada-bing bada-boom," this program would continue, writing a story up to 1,000 words in length. The computer would ask for elaboration if the elements were not clear, then the screen would split and the text would begin to scroll up the left side while graphics illustrated the story on the right.

The story would be labeled "Untitled First Draft" with the day, hour, and minute of completion and the location of the computer. A hard copy would be printed with supporting graphics, and a copy of the whole thing would be filed by e-mail with the Writers Guild of America and the Copyright Office.

Dooley started with his own large disk library of classic stories from Aesop, Beatrix Potter, Rafael Sabatini, Victor Hugo, and deMaupassant to Nordhoff and Hall, Patrick O'Brian, and Ian Fleming. The player could also select an option to create a musical score for the story. Dooley also had most of the world's popular and great classical music on CD, which he loaded onto the hard disk with BadaBing BadaBoom. [Note to Beavis: "classical" means Mozart, not The Beatles.]

The player's selection process was cumbersome at first. When Floyd Turner, Dooley's assistant on the program, was given the honor of creating the first story, he punched Plot and wrote

> **Three old men go fishing for sharks,**
> **get scared,**
> **catch one,**
> **eat lunch,**
> **drink beer,**
> **tell dumb stories,**
> **talk about bossy women,**
> **come home.**

The computer translated this as

> **Male-Bonding Adventure/Comedy**

and asked

Saltwater or fresh?
What kind of boat?

Floyd answered

Salt
42' trawler

Under "Characters," Floyd named

Grumpy: Captain/Owner, stutters
LT: one-armed, wears pistol
Hendry: tells story about great white shark a lot
Nanny: Grumpy's wife, does not actually appear
Azul Viejo: the villain, a big evil shark

Under "Other Elements," he typed

Time: Present, 8 a.m. to 4 p.m., on a sunny day
Place: San Pedro Harbor and south ten miles
Sex: 0
Violence: Fish get hurt. Azul shot and captured.

Under "Music," Floyd put

Boat adventure music

The computer chose parts of *The Theme From Jaws*, *The Theme From Mutiny on the Bounty*, and *The Good Ship Lollipop*.

Under "Activities," Floyd typed

Speak a little Spanish, eat hot chili, drink beer, and say some dumb things.

Dooley concluded at this point that Floyd had been on a lot of fishing trips.

Under "Length of Story," Floyd selected the maximum

1,000 words

Finally the "Ready" light came on and Floyd, Dooley, Juanita-Maria, Bud, Jeffrey, and I, together with a handful of test pilots, watched the story unroll.

Writing is harder
than pushing a button and
seeing what comes out.

Once upon a time there was an old salt named Grumpy who lived on his boat, Misty IV. That's where Grumpy lived because his wife, Nanny, suffered from a rare disease called *folie de bâtir*, which caused her to hire cretinous workmen who would tear down, rebuild, promise to arrive, not arrive, hammer, hammer, hammer, bang, bang, bang on her house. All that commotion gave Grumpy a big headache. So he lived on his boat, Misty IV.

One day Grumpy started Misty's engines, disconnected the electric power cord and telephone wire, checked all those important things that make Nanny's eyes cross with boredom, and then cast off the mooring lines. With his friends LT (who has only one arm), Hendry, twelve beers, and a big pot of chili, he guided Misty out of her slip, round the corner past the fuel dock, and on out past the breakwater. Anyone who happened to look over the port quarter as Misty rounded the entrance buoy and headed out to sea might have noticed a long, dark shape gliding past, its upturned eye unblinking, fixed menacingly on Misty and her staunch crew.

As the three comrades headed seaward, they drank beer and talked of famous shark encounters. Hendry told of the great white he'd caught off the Ventura breeding grounds. Grumpy spoke of his adventure with the notorious lemon sharks of the Caribbean who love to bite off fishermen's hands when they trail their fingers in the water. Then Hendry told of his great white shark again because he liked that story better than Grumpy's.

"Did you lose your arm to a great white, LT?" asked Grumpy in an effort to keep Hendry from telling his story for the third time.

"No," said LT, "I lost it in the divorce settlement after my first marriage."

"I wonder who her lawyer was," mused Nanny when she heard this story later.

LT and Hendry tied the green and white salmon flies on the fishing lines and trolled them behind the boat.

Whompf! Whompf! Almost immediately they were struck by two bonitos who fought the fishermen all the way into the boat. Soon there were thirty or thirty-five mackerel and bonito swimming around in the live bait tank, where water is continuously pumped in from the sea and overflows back to keep the bait moderately happy and lively.

"Hey, Grumpy!" said LT, sticking his head in the wheelhouse, "We've got enough bait in the tank; let's stop and see if we can catch a shark!" At this moment, if anyone had been looking, they'd have seen an ominous swirl on the starboard beam.

Grumpy went back to the bait tank and, seizing bonito and mackerel indiscriminately, hacked them to ribbons with his rusty knife and threw the mutilated fish back into the bait tank. The overflow turned bright red and a slick of bloody water, irresistible to sharks, spread outward from the Misty.

"Good work, Grumpy!" said LT, "Your color's better and I notice you've stopped stuttering!"

LT and Grumpy selected heavy fishing rods and attached braided wire leaders to the lines. Next, a few lead sinkers and a shark hook were rigged. Now each fisherman selected a lively bonito from among those left unmaimed by Grumpy in his blood-slick operation and impaled it on his shark hook.

Meanwhile, Hendry was pulling up rockfish from the bottom 360 feet below. He was cleverly using an eight-ounce sinker and six cod hooks, each one with a small piece of squid on it for bait.

"Struggling fish," said Hendry. "That's what attracts sharks. Did I ever tell you about the great white I caught off the Ventura breeding grounds?"

"Think I'll make lunch," said Grumpy, for it is a well-known fact that fishermen get cranky if they don't eat promptly at noon. Soon three heads were bent low and five elbows were in the air over three steaming bowls of fragrant chili, topped with chopped onions and grated cheese.

"Mas queso y cebollas, por favor," said Hendry, for it is also well-known that good fishermen speak only Spanish while eating.

"¿Si como no?" said LT, passing the dishes one at a time. "I think I'll go check the baits." As Grumpy moved to the galley to wash the dishes as Nanny had trained him to do, there was a sudden shout from LT.

"Hey, look what's over here on the port side! We're gonna need a bigger boat!" There, cruising alongside, one eye balefully fixed on Misty's meaty crew, was an eight-foot long blue shark!

"That's Azul Viejo!" said Hendry. "He's claimed many a gringo skin!"

"But he hasn't reckoned with me," said Grumpy, as the shark swallowed his bonito in one gulp and took off for Hawaii.

After a long fight, the thrashing fish loomed out of the sea. He was beating the water to foam with his tail while shaking his head in rage, rolling his bloodshot eyes, and baring his many rows of teeth! LT, fearing for everyone's safety, slipped his trusty .22 pistol out of its well-worn breakaway holster.

Blam! Blam! Blam! Nine times he shot Azul Viejo in the head.

"That won't kill him," said Hendry, "but it might ruin his whole day."

Warily, Grumpy brought the shark to the swimstep. Working carefully and
    skillfully, LT and Hendry got the flying gaff fixed in the shark's mouth and
    a loop around his tail. Wham! There was Azul Viejo, trussed up like a
    bull on the swimstep!
As Misty chugged back with her grim cargo still rolling his eyes on the
    swimstep and her happy crew gurgling their fourth beers in celebration,
    anyone with sharp ears would have heard Hendry say, "I recall one day,
    off the Ventura breeding grounds…"

THE END

Fishing is fun, but
only because it's scary
and then safe at last.

Hendry, Azul, and LT with Misty IV.
Photo by Grumpy

AUDIENCE REACTION

After everyone had read and seen Floyd's story, we passed out rating cards. This was their average rating of the various characters.

Likability 0 (low) to 10 (high)

Grumpy	*3*
LT	*4*
Hendry	*2*
Nanny	*9*
Azul Viejo	*10*

It was decided that the numbers weren't good enough to call for a sequel.

Dooley's reaction was to build in a holograph option so that the player could find out more about the characters in the story. When Juanita-Maria tested the game later, she called up Floyd's story and then punched "Holograph: Autobio." When the CRT asked "Which character?" Juanita-Maria typed "Nanny" and up on the screen came a holographic image of Nanny, who delivered her "Autobio" as follows.

This "scientific marketing" is certainly an oxymoron.

NANNY'S CAMEO

"Don't get me wrong," Nanny's holograph said, "Grumpy and I have had a lot of good years together. It's just that I've outlasted the old bugger—that's all.

"After we got married in San Diego, it was World War II. He was about to be shipped off to a destroyer in the Aleutian Islands, and I was pregnant.

"Later we lived on Long Island and he commuted to Wall Street an hour and a half each way, while I raised five children. In the evening I'd be tired of baby-talk and baby-think and need some adult conversation. He'd been in a battle of wits all day and needed a couple of stiff drinks, a roll in the hay, and lights out.

"When he retired, the kids were grown and gone, and we moved to San Pedro. I was ready for travel, challenge, anything. Trouble was, Grumpy's get-up-and-go had got up and gone.

"So he's got Misty IV and his buddies LT, Hendry and an old blind dog who staggers around the fuel dock. I've got regular bridge and tennis, and the five children are my best friends. Mercifully, they've all inherited the sense of comedy that's kept Grumpy and me together all these years.

"Speaking of which, our fiftieth anniversary is coming up in a few months and I'd like to renew our vows in church and invite the children and our close friends to take part in the ceremony. Grumpy says he'll elope to Las Vegas for the weekend, but that's all the ritual he can handle.

"Oh well. Mustn't grumble. I've been to London to visit our British daughter who is now a Sioux Indian living in Ojai. I've been scuba diving in Kailua-Kona with our Hawaiian son. I've been to the south of France with our lawyer daughter, to Nepal with our Buddhist daughter, and to Wales and Ireland with my sister. I'm planning a trip now, and I'll check Grumpy into the Pritikin Longevity Institute for 26 days while I'm gone. Although why he should be interested in longevity with his attitude is beyond me.

Tant pis, as they say in Provence when they aren't saying *merde*.

DOOLEY GETS A KITCHEN

It seemed to me that Dooley was getting a little snappish and looking a bit harried, so we took a break and went for a walk.

Dooley was never a complainer; it turned out that he was working on so many things and enjoying it so much that he had no time to prepare meals and eat. Dooley had never liked restaurants. "As soon as you teach one to work without cholesterol, fat, sugar, and salt, it goes broke and you have to start over."

"Suppose I set up the room in back of the third storefront as a real kitchen and get some volunteer test pilots to sign on as your chefs? I'll help them get organized. It will be awful at first, but maybe something good will come out of it. What do you think? Your call." Dooley was game, so I put out a call for volunteers to be chefs in Dooley's new kitchen.

This time we only got seven volunteers, so I sent Dooley back to work and we had our first kitchen cabinet meeting. All the equipment had been ordered. It was going to be installed and checked out over the balance of the week. Next Monday would be the start of their new careers.

105

The work was divided into seven parts.

Meal planning
Shopping and buying
Inventory (keeping track of the money, receipts, and food on hand)
Preparing food
Cooking food
Continuous cleaning
A utility chef or troubleshooter, so to speak, who could fill in where needed

I suggested they draw straws to see who got what job and that they change jobs every two weeks so they would each learn the whole operation. If anybody hated their work, they shouldn't sulk but instead should call a staff meeting and discuss it. If anybody quit, it was up to the group to decide whether to bring in another person and, if so, who; if not, they'd have to decide how to split up the work among the remaining chefs.

The meal-planner chef and I worked out the following menu, which Dooley was stuck with until we were able to start working on variations.

*Breakfast: Oatmeal, cinnamon, raisins, banana, grapefruit, nonfat
    milk, Colombian coffee*

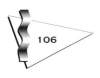

Lunch: Huge chopped salad of cucumbers, tomatoes, red peppers, carrots, lettuce, celery, onion powder, white pepper, Paula's No-Oil Orange and Basil dressing, lemon
Dinner: Lima beans, baked potato, frozen leaf spinach, frozen broccoli, melon, lemon

We gave this list to the shopping and buying chef and when she returned we worked with the preparing chef. The cooking chef helped out because there wasn't much for him to do that first week. We were working between 3 p.m. and 6 p.m., and all we could do was wash the vegetables and prepare the potato for baking and the frozen vegetables for steaming. Then we chopped the salad for tomorrow's lunch, covered it, and put it in the refrigerator.

Within a week Dooley was looking and feeling much better and was tired enough of his new diet to ask his chefs to make smaller and more frequent meals.

The staff persuaded Dooley to play ThunderBuns to see what he would look like in two years on a diet of steak, eggs, hash browns, cheese, cookies, peanut butter, and ice cream. They agreed he looked like Bluto.

Used to be women's work; now it's a job for the whole fam damily.

DOOLEY'S DINER

Dooley is so healthy I asked him to write up an eating plan. He said he already had one in the computer for people like me who thought they could overcome a lifetime of bad habits with a week of austerity.

"How old are you, Dooley?" I asked him.

"Thirty-eight."

"What made you take this eating and aerobics track?"

"I used to eat and drink and sit around like you do. But after a heart attack at 20, a triple bypass at 22, and a stroke at 25, I got the feeling nature was trying to tell me something. So I checked into the Pritikin Longevity Center in Santa Monica for 26 days and discovered what I'm about to hand you."

He punched something up on the computer and printed out a hard copy that looked like this.

LIMIT—Cholesterol, fat, sugar, sodium, refined carbohydrates.
Cholesterol: less than 100 mg. per day.
Fat: 10% of calories.

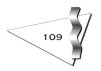

109

Sugar (jam): 2 tbs per day. (Remember: honey, syrup, lactose, fructose, dextrose, anything-ose, and refined and concentrated fruit juices all contain sugar.)

Sodium: 1,600 mg. per day or 1 mg. per calorie on refined products.

Animal protein: 3 $\frac{1}{2}$ oz. per day (think of it as a garnish on your plate like parsley).

The number of complex carbohydrate servings plus the number of fruit servings should equal the number of vegetable servings (cooked and uncooked), or CC + F = V. Eat the whole fruit. Juicing removes the fiber.

STOP—Animal fats, tropical oils, and processed oils (especially hydrogenated), butter, lard, margarine. Stop fatty meats, organ meats, processed meats, whole and lowfat dairy, cheeses (except nonfat ricotta), egg yolks, deep-fried anything, cookies, cakes, nondairy whipped toppings, rich desserts.

CAUTION—Avocados, olives, nuts, sugar-free or fat-free desserts, olive oil, canola oil, peanut oil, safflower oil, sunflower oil, corn oil (They have no cholesterol or animal fat, but they all have FAT!)

EAT—Five, six, or seven small meals a day (under 300 calories each). Never gorge or binge, but, on the other hand NEVER GET HUNGRY!

ALCOHOL—No more than 7 glasses of wine per week (2 per day max) OR 3 drinks of hard liquor per week (2 per day max).

EATING OUT—Visit your favorite restaurants and ask the manager (not the host or hostess) to help you out. Tell him or her you want to keep dining there but you'll die right at the table if you have any fat, salt, or sugar. Any restaurant worth its name can sauté a half chicken breast in tomato, onion, basil, garlic, and white wine. Ask for the papaya sauce on your poached salmon instead of the tarragon beurre blanc. Visit other restaurants and use "medical reasons" to get their attention. Dine at 6:00 p.m. or 8:30 p.m. when they're less busy.

Eat a salad, a piece of fruit, or half a head of lettuce before you go out to dinner. Don't worry about the amount of oil in a normal marinara sauce. Take a vial of oat bran and another vial of oil-free low sodium dressing with you. When eating white rice or refined pasta sprinkle some oat bran on it, thereby adding back the fiber that has been lost in refining. Order your salad without dressing and use your own.

EXERCISE—45 to 60 minutes per day, 6 days per week. Stretch before and after.

STRESS—Take a short time out several times a day. Relax eyebrows, neck, and back. Take 3 to 10 deep breaths and drink some water.

Read labels; buy right
stuff; eat right; a month later
your taste buds will change.

LEE NA PING AND THE MARTIAL ARTS

Archibald came to visit us in April.

"When the school year ends, what are you going to do with all these storefronts?"

"Shut them all down except one and get Dooley's kitchen, apartment, and lab all into that unit."

"Want a suggestion about one of the other storefronts?"

"Sure."

"The greatest teacher of aikido in the world and an old friend of mine from the CBI theater *[that's China, Burma, India, Butt-Head]* is a chef in a Chinese restaurant in San Pedro. He's 73 and not looking forward to a summer in an un-air-conditioned kitchen. If you set him up with an apartment, an office, some mats and uniforms for the big room, and a modest salary, he could teach the philosophy and practice of self-defense free to a lot of kids this summer.

"We don't want to make samurai warriors out of our kids," said Dooley. "There are enough gangs out there now."

"Don't worry," said Archibald. "Get Lee to explain aikido when you interview him."

Dooley and I interviewed Lee Na Ping the next afternoon. We were happy when he accepted our offer, and ecstatic when he jumped for joy at the idea of cooking occasional fat-free, oil-free, salt-free, sugar-free, MSG-free meals in Dooley's air-conditioned kitchen.

In answer to Dooley's question about teaching violence, Lee offered to meet us tomorrow in my reading room.

You don't make friends, you recognize them. Lee Na Ping was a friend of ours.

AIKIDO

"Don't worry about violence, Dooley," said Lee Na Ping. "Aikido is the purest of the defensive martial arts. You are trained to calm yourself and become very alert and watchful. And you never fight in anger, nor do you ever attack. Think about that.

"The essence of aikido is *yawara*, which means yielding or giving way. You use your own alertness, calmness, and speed to turn the attacker's momentum against him.

"I will be teaching the kids the first stage of aikido, which is called *shojin.* This means using your will and consciousness to learn technique. It usually takes three years, and I'll be teaching on three levels: The *wasa*, or technique; the *tai*, or body, grace, speed and strength; and the *shin*, the mind or spirit.

"The second stage, which is only reached by serious students with at least three years of *shojin*, is called *shiho*, and it's when the mind and body have mastered the technique so well that reactions are instinctive and instantaneous. This is necessary because in a real-life attack, you can't count on having any warning or time to think."

119

"Are you a black belt, Lee?" I asked.

"Fifth Dan in aikido," replied Lee, "but I've been practicing for 65 years, and I've still got a long way to go. Don't worry, gentlemen, none of our kids will ever regret time spent practicing aikido."

Grace, balance, speed, with a calm mind, unblinkingly alert = aikido.

JUANITA-MARIA CONQUERS FRENCH AND ITALIAN

Perhaps because she sensed our doubts, Juanita-Maria continued her linguistic quest, even though she'd handily won the contest.

Un deux trois quatre cinq six sept huit neuf dix.

Comment tu vas? Ça va.

C'est quoi, ton nom? M'appelle Juanita-Maria Francesca.

Pourquoi tu manges cette merde? Tu vas devenir vieux, gras, et décrépi. Si tu veux voir a quoi tu va resembler, viens avec moi au centre et joues une partie de "ThunderBuns" avec nous.

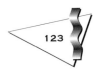

123

Uno due tre quattro cinque sei sette otto nove dieci.

Come va? A me va bene.

Come ti chiami? Io mi chiamo Juanita-Maria Francesca.

Perche mangii quella porcheria? Ti va diventare vecchio, grasso e brutto. Si vuoi veder ti sembri, vieni con me alla centrale a fare una partita di "ThunderBuns."

We felt terrible for doubting her.

Speaking foreign tongues
is much better learned early.
Age destroys the knack.

COORDINATES:
Accounting Department
Fritz Braunschweiger
Controller
NO. OF EMPLOYEES: 21
COMPANY: Droids R Us
CEO: Sterling Mentor
AGE: 45
AVERAGE ENERGY
LEVEL—COMPANY
GOAL: SW-2
QUERY: What is the
goal of the
department?
What is the
average energy
level toward the
goal of the
department?

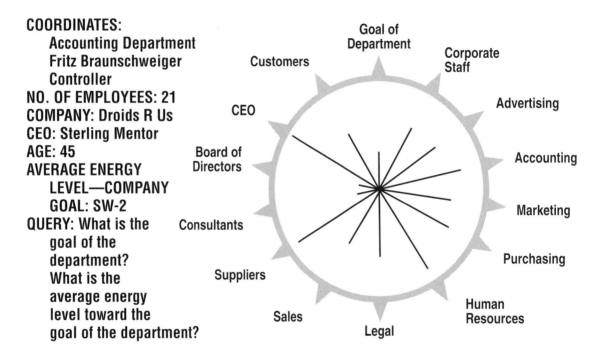

126

GOAL OF DEPARTMENT: To get the monthly financials to the CEO and corporate staff by the twentieth working day of the following month come hell or high water and whether we understand the numbers or not.

EVALUATION: This was an early QVT success. When people saw the goal they were stunned. All it required was that Mr. Mentor, the CEO, suggest to Mr. Braunschweiger that a more useful goal would be: "ASAP get the monthly financials to the operating division heads, the corporate staff, and the CEO with a one-page cover interpreting the data and calling attention to any unusual or nonrecurring factors." This change was made with relief and enthusiasm, and the effectiveness of the Controller's Accounting Department improved to SW-5.

COORDINATES:
   Marketing Department
   Brad Brady
   V.P.
COMPANY: Cyborg City
NO. OF EMPLOYEES: 31
CEO: Samuel Shiftee
AGE: 67
AVERAGE
   ENERGY LEVEL —
   COMPANY
   GOAL: FW-3
QUERY: How is this
   department
   allocating its energy?

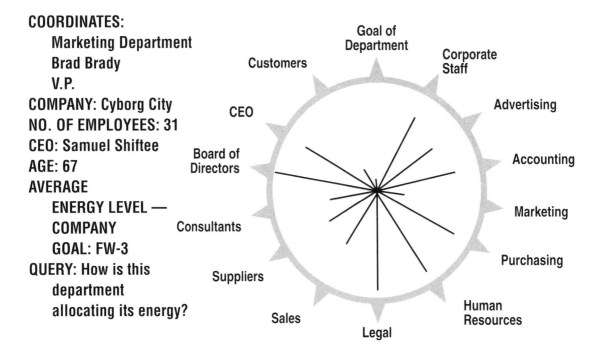

EVALUATION: This was one of the conclusive early discoveries that not all marketing departments are usefully employed. Jobs were found for everyone in other areas of the company, and the function of marketing was taken over by the CEO and the sales department.

KARMATRON

One day Dooley and Lee were up in my reading room enjoying their beverages of choice: Dooley, fresh grapefruit juice; Lee, Green Magma. I had leaded coffee with powdered nonfat milk.

"Lee," I asked, "What do you know about Buddhism?"

Lee did not reply immediately, but savored his Green Magma for a moment, and then looked over at me.

"The Buddhists have a very succinct view of the way we North Americans live," answered Lee. "They call it "cyclic existence" and it's symbolized in their iconography as a pig (ignorance) chasing a rooster (greed) chasing a snake (hatred) chasing the pig."

"That sounds like where I used to work," I said.

"I figured you'd recognize that part," said Lee, "Let's see how you do with reincarnation and karma. To a Buddhist, we three must have purified our consciousness considerably in past lives because we've made out like bandits in this one. The question, to paraphrase what Marley said to Scrooge, is 'How are we doing with our karma in this life, as that will impact what we come back as in the next?'"

"What exactly does karma mean?" I asked.

131

"Well, I'm no *rinpoche,* but to me karma is one of the most misunderstood of Eastern concepts. Westerners think it means fate or destiny; it really means almost the opposite—cause and effect. The belief is that we're all living a series of connected lives, and the quality of each life is determined by the goodness and compassion of our thought and action in the previous one. The driving principle is that we are not predestined. We can improve our lives by feeling a sense of oneness with humanity and other sentient beings, and acting accordingly. As Thomas More said, 'We are all in the same cart traveling toward execution; how can I feel anger or wish harm to anyone else?'"

"Sheesh, Lee," said Dooley, "You're a long-winded old geezer. Karma means "action" and it's the force behind reincarnation. You will be reborn in a form that reflects your actions in your previous life."

"You can't believe in this stuff, Dooley," I said, "You're a mathematician!"

"If you define believing as 'admitting the possibility of,'" said Dooley, "I'm a believer."

I took a sip of leaded coffee and thought for a moment.

"Lee," I said, summoning my courage, "What is the worst that can happen if I die leaving a lot of highly toxic karmic waste behind?"

"Let's see...if you were miserly, you might come back into poverty. If you were arrogant, you'll be put into a situation that necessitates humility. There are any number of possibilities. One of the shortcomings of modern life is that we've grown so accustomed to immediate gratification and instant responses that we feel, if we have privileges, that we must be doing something right. But in the karmic doctrine, you may have done something right a long time ago and only now be reaping the benefits. Later, you'll reap what you are currently sowing. It's like a cosmic time-lag."

For a few moments they sat and did nothing. But it didn't last.

"Dooley," I said, "Is there a game emerging here? Could we create a kind of ThunderBuns for the spirit? Project what are likely to be the future incarnations of players according to their thoughts and actions this go-round?"

Dooley was reluctant to play Brahma, but he did have another idea gestating. At last it emerged.

"When I was young, the big threat that assured us our angst was nuclear war; today it's the destruction of the environment—the kids can identify with that. We could design a game, call it KarmaTron or something, to project the future results of our present ecological habits.

"Assume that each player represents a hundred million Americans. A decision to eat one hamburger a week could be translated into the number of acres of rain forest burned to provide cattle with grazing land for that extra beef and the growth of extra trash from the fast-food chains. We could incorporate a digital doomsday clock to show how many days the human species has left to live based on various possible decisions. And we could build in some cool graphics to show what parts of the planet would look like if certain decisions are made. I should be able to download assorted computer graphics as part of the database and take it from there."

It won the instant approval of our rooftop triumvirate. We brainstormed and e-mailed people we respected. Juanita-Maria, Jeffrey, Floyd, and Bud were with us every afternoon from 3 p.m. to 6 p.m. for the next few weeks. Their input was golden; after all, they would be the primary players of the game and the inheritors of the planet.

We brought in Archibald, who had access to the facts and theories of the mainstreamers all the way from the hard-line techno-optimists to the wild-eyed catastrophists. I represented the not-in-my-lifetime eco-morons, Dooley was a solid Green, and the kids were more ready for change than we expected. We invited the mayor of San Pedro to join us on behalf of the NIMBYists.

Most of the major environmental problems got into the game: greenhouse effect, air pollution, ozone depletion, vanishing rain forest, arable land loss, hazardous waste, acid rain, soil salinization, groundwater pollution, ocean and beach pollution, vanishing species, vanishing water table, and mounting garbage to name a few.

Then we dealt with the human attempts to ameliorate the damage: recycling and reusing, canvas and string shopping bags, bottles in toilet tanks, less driving, more carpooling, more walking and biking, less red meat, grants to build homes out of old tires, petitioning utilities to convert to solar and wind power, and so on.

But mostly Dooley worked on the graphics. We figured that the environmentalists had brought the issue to the first page of the national agenda, bless their hearts, and KarmaTron might administer some shock treatment. Dooley was great working with the animators after he stopped trying to get them to cooperate and assigned each team a project of their own choosing. They really delivered the goods; hardly a day passed that the kids were not treated to a new graphic horror show. Even Hieronymus Bosch would have been proud.

When we had agreed on all the elements of the game, Dooley started writing code. I should point out that Dooley writes code like nobody else.

He has a vast store of software in his removable optical disk library. Beyond that, he has access to anything out there. But the real secret to Dooley's speed is that he knows where whole cathedrals of code are, and he puts them together in chunks. He can assemble chunks of code that nobody ever tried to connect before. He even has a program that works testing interfaces while he sleeps the four hours he needs every day.

Anyway, nobody was surprised when KarmaTron was created, born, tested, and debugged two weeks later. The graphics were primitive compared with what we have today, but the game still packed a wallop.

As the house eco-jerk I was allowed the first try.

The game started with a questionnaire.

1. Do you have water bottles in your toilet tanks?
2. Are your tires properly inflated?
3. Do you make a sincere effort to drive 10% less?
4. On a scale of one-to-ten, how much do you recycle cans, newspaper, plastic, paper, glass, and batteries?
5. Do you reuse plastic containers?

And so on...

My answers produced dismal planetary effect graphics, a doomsday clock that said we had three months left, and a Stimpy-like cartoon of my face on a baby seal strangling with a plastic six-pack ring around its neck.

I was, perhaps, a little defensive.

"I know I know, gimme a break. There's nothing worse than a reformed smoker, drunkard, or enviro-slob. But those graphics really got to me." My imitation of Alistair Sim playing Scrooge was sublime: "I'm not the man I was! Let's do something!"

In the end we took a few practical measures and felt that, on balance, KarmaTron would be a valuable contribution.

1. We gave everybody a canvas bag and a couple of string bags. That's easy: it's a relief not to have all those paper and plastic bags nagging at your conscience.
2. We started the "Change-of-the-Month" at the test center. The kids picked "No Styrofoam Anything!" as the first project.
3. We started an e-mail newsletter on efforts/results.
4. We invited world leaders and assorted followers to play KarmaTron (and ThunderBuns).

5. Archibald called his short list of enlightened CEOs and we e-mailed all of our QVT subscribers: would they consider asking all their people to spend one work hour out of a 40-hour week working to preserve the environment in whatever way would be most effective and satisfying to each individual. So far a dozen or so are trying it, and the QVT people are measuring the effect on energy and focus. Early results are promising.

More human being
and less human doing would
let Earth heal itself.

THE A LIST

Some of Dooley's best games came out of the Bummer Loop he built into all the games. If you had a problem at school or at home and wanted to spew, as Juanita-Maria would say, you pressed the Bummer Button. You would be connected to the Bummer Box on Dooley's worktable. Your screen would read:

So tell me!

One day Dooley caught a squeal from Floyd Turner. His old man's back surgery wasn't accepted by Medicare, which said his premiums weren't paid. Cisco Turner was over 70, and for some months the premiums had been paid directly by Social Security and deducted from his monthly benefits.

Dooley and I called Archibald. After our telephone conference, we dumped the CD-ROM files of Archibald's 12 yellow phone books into our mainframe. Using Cisco Turner's back surgery as a test, we punched up

Social Security Administration

and got ten pages of names, titles, and direct-dial phone numbers.

"Bingo!" said Dooley.

At random, we picked an executive assistant,* Felicita Carter, in the Commissioner's office, and dialed her number in Baltimore. She listened to Cisco's problem, took down his name, address, and social security number, and explained what was going to happen.

"This goes on all the time. We tell people to stop paying premiums on Medicare because at age 70 we start paying them and then another part of the system cuts off their benefits for nonpayment. Neat, isn't it? This is what we're gonna do. Tell Cisco to stop filing claims until we call him to tell him the glitch is fixed. This is handled in San Francisco, which is responsible for San Pedro. Our computers in Baltimore don't interface with San Francisco, so I'll telephone Melanie there, explain the deal, and she'll call you at the test center within 24 hours."

---

* In this case you are looking for the sergeants who work the particular network you need. Not the privates or corporals, and certainly not the brigadiers or majors or captains. You'll get better at finding them with practice.

The next day Melanie called.

"It'll take about 30 days to fix this. I'll call you when it's done and then Mr. Turner can send all his claims in. I know how frustrating this is, especially because his supplementary insurance won't pay until Medicare pays, and poor Mr. Turner is sitting there with no help in sight. Tell him to relax. Melanie is on his case now."

Less than a month later Melanie called to say everything was cool, Cisco filed his claims, Medicare paid about 40%, and the supplementary paid the balance without a whimper.

"You have to remember," said Archibald when we told him the network of his yellow phone books was working fine, "most people in Washington and government employees in general are like the Maytag repairman in the television ad. They love to help; it's what they're there for; if only you can get to them. What you have in your mainframe now is the way to get to the right person fast. Congratulations!"

And that's how the Bummer Button gave us a whole new game which we started calling "Archibald's 300,000 Friends," then "The Yellow Files," then "Access to Action," and finally "The A List."

Bureaucrats want to
help; the big trick is to get
the right person first.

THE COMPOUND

Our storefronts formed a compound and looked like this:

EXPANDED GAME ROOM	ORIGINAL GAME ROOM (DOOLEY'S APT. UPSTAIRS; CRUNCH'S READING ROOM ON ROOF.)	DOOLEY'S OFFICE	
		DOOLEY'S KITCHEN (LEE NA PING'S APT. ABOVE)	
		DOOLEY'S LAB (AIKIDO CENTER ABOVE)	
STOREFRONT ON THE OTHER SIDE	ORIGINAL STOREFRONT	STOREFRONT NEXT DOOR	

(Crunch moved his reading room to the roof of the Aikido Center in anticipation of the other storefronts being closed for summer vacation.)

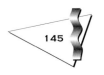

145

GRASSE MATINÉE

Game: Klass Klown
Type of dance, music, or song: Noel Coward/Franglais
Feeling: Deliciously lazy
Story: Lady sleeps until noon and has breakfast in bed

Every day's a *grasse matinée*
When my baby has *thé complet;*
First a *croissant*, then a *petit-pain,*
All the rest of the morning
In the *salle de bain.*

Oh, every day's a *grasse matinée*
When my baby has *thé complet*
Hey hey,
When my baby has *thé complet.*

147

SLURP!

"It continually amazes me," said Archibald, "that it has never occurred to any of the advantaged kids I know to figure out how to tap the money rivers out of Washington.* Congress has started programs for years but never learned how to stop them. The money is there for the taking; why don't we make a game out of it, Crunch? I could set up channels of rough data to you in San Pedro, but it wouldn't be easily accessible. Do you suppose Dooley could take bunches of unorganized data from lots of sources and organize it?"

*According to Archibald, much of the value in Washington of course is not the rivers of money but the human repositories of up-to-date information. The fact that it is free if you can find it is matched by the willingness with which it is given. He asks:

"Would you rather talk to your doctor about your recently discovered prostate cancer or breast cancer and wonder how many recent issues of the *New England Journal of Medicine* he hasn't gotten around to reading, or to the doctor in the National Institutes of Health who has been working on prostate cancer or breast cancer for six years, has assembled all the knowledge in one databank and has written the last five monographs, which he will happily send you for free?

"Would you rather hire a lawyer to draw up a franchise agreement for you (while he's learning on your nickel) or would you rather talk for free to the lawyer in the Federal Trade Commission who drafted the franchise law and knows all the loopholes the lobbyists later put in, as well as all the pros and cons of all the clauses, and will gladly mail you lots of stuff?"

149

"Let's ask him."

So Dooley came up to the roof, and SLURP! was born.

Before they made the game available to the kids, Crunch and Dooley asked Archibald whether he thought it was the right thing to do or not. "Listen," said Archibald, "government has become a game. It's called 'How much harm are we going to do in this effort to do good?' There's no reason taxpayers can't reply with something like this game, which is really asking 'How much money can we siphon off to people who are legally entitled to it under your asinine regulations?'"

When a kid started to play, SLURP! would get his attention by asking

Did you know you can probably nail the government for megabucks every month? Want to hear more?

When a kid said "Y," the machine started to ask questions until the kid hit "Enter," which meant "This is the right area."

The machine would ask more questions, and when it had enough data, it might, for example, say:

You are entitled to compensation under HR902, children of unemployed left-handed parents with one or more psychic disabilities. Would you like me to fill in Form 1-9027-94, write a cover letter of transmittal, and print a hard copy for your signature?

Archibald set up a continuous flow of unorganized material from Washington, Dooley organized it and made it accessible in San Pedro, and Crunch paid the tab.

In 1999, the GAO reported a significant shift of entitlement payments to the San Pedro, California, area.

So what can be wrong
with being a player in
the world's biggest game?

THE ROOF

Yesterday I was on the roof of the storefront reading the new Elmore Leonard when Dooley came busting through the door.

"Crunch," he said, "I need some help."

"Blast it, Dooley, you know I hate getting hauled into your daily foul-ups."

"Listen, Chief, if there were any place else to go, don't you think I'd go there? You are such a pain to deal with when you're up here."

"Well, that's a good start. How can this humble pain be of service to Your Royal Technosity?"

It turned out that Juanita-Maria, Dooley's ace mechanic, was going through a bad patch and Dooley wanted the two of us to talk to her and see if we could find a way to help.

"Juanita-Maria's one of our best. If we can't help her, this whole project is in danger."

So she came up to my sacred reading area, which was fast becoming a day-care center in my eyes.

"Crunch," said Juanita-Maria, "I mean, what do I want with being up

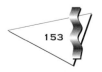

153

here, spewing to you? No offense, but like no way can a wheezebag like you help me out."

After a half-hour of wading through a morass of Valleyspeak, it turned out that she had developed a tremendous anxiety about the rest of her life and had become panicky about the choices she was making every day.

"Welcome to the club, Juanita-Maria," I said. "We've all been there. But why can't His Royal Technosity over there work on some kind of game that helps us explore our options and choices? An interactive whaddyacallit."

"Not going to be easy, Crunch. I'll need some help laying out the problems and choices and consequences," offered Dooley. Juanita-Maria grinned.

"Whoa. Like, a game that'll tell me what to do? Cool..."

"No, a game that will tell all of us what's likely to happen when we make certain choices. You'll still have to choose what you want to do."

"Oh. Bummer."

And that is how Rat Race was born. It was an entire week before I finished my Elmore Leonard novel.

Peace comes with a good reading room. Ample reward for years of hard work.

RAT RACE

During that week, I suppose I didn't miss Elmore because I was learning so much from Dooley.

"Work," said Dooley, "is the key to happiness. I don't mean work-work. I mean fun work. If you enjoy your work and get paid to do it, you are on the right path.

"The kids we've been working with scare me. They remind me of me, and that reminds me of how lucky I was. They're like boats without radar in a thick fog: no idea which way to turn; no idea how much danger lies where.

"Juanita-Maria's not the only kid who's worried. Maybe this Rat Race game I'm working on will help."

"What are you going to put in it, Dooley?"

"The concepts of 'Stretch' and 'Fetch,' and the effect of choices measured in time and money. Also, the education requirements that go along with each strategy.

"The object of the game is to plan your life so you get as much Stretchtime as possible. My life, like everybody else's, starts with 168

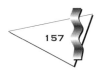

157

hours a week. Out of that some time expenditures are fixed: sleep 49 hours; food acquisition, preparation, and eating 20 hours; fitness 7.5 hours; maintenance/paperwork 1.5 hours; that's a total of 78 hours gone, leaving 90 hours.

"Now comes the variable of commuting. In my case that's an hour a week because I live where I work. If someone lived in Moreno Valley and worked in Santa Monica she'd have a 3-hour round-trip commute 5 days a week or 15 hours. In my case I'm down to 89 hours available for Fetch and Stretch. Fetch pays the bills, and Stretch is getting better at what I enjoy doing, and in my case they're one and the same, so I'm home free with 89 hours of Stretchtime.

"Ms. Moreno Valley hates her job, so 40 hours a week becomes pure Fetch, and she's down to 35 hours a week. If she's married, she'll spend 10 hours a week with her spouse without the kids, and at least 10 hours a week with the kids and pets, so she's down to 15 hours a week. If the time with spouse and kids and pets is pure Stretch, that's fine, but if the spouse is griping about life in Moreno Valley and the kids are squalling and dirty, she'll probably spend her 15 hours bowling, playing bridge, or drinking. That's not a happy choice for any of them. But it's an option.

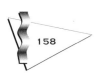

"On a happier note, Rat Race could give some valuable advice to the lucky few who are going to make it in professional sports or entertainment, like

>Your career may be short, so save half of your money after taxes from day one. Put it in a large, highly regarded mutual fund group. Don't give it to your business manager to invest.

"To get back to reality, let's say Rat Race starts with the question

>How much education are you going to get?
>Post-grad degree
>College degree
>Community college degree
>High school diploma or equivalency
>Less than that

"If someone punches in 'Less than that,' Rat Race will say:

>Waiter/Waitress, Home Cleaner, Receptionist, Host/Hostess, Bartender, Hairdresser, Car Wash Attendant, Quick-Lube Trainee, Supermarket Bagger or Checker

Your earning power today is $250 per week max. That's $1,125 a
month. Withholding knocks off $225, so you take home $900.
Share an apartment, pay no more than $200 rent per month. The
rest of your budget is $700. Here's how you might spend it.

Chow	$200
Telephone	200
Cable TV	25
Clothes	70
Health Insurance	105
Gimme a Break Fund	100
Total	$700

$100 a month for movies, CDs, rock concerts, and snacks is cutting it
thin.

"That's not a bad start," said Dooley. "Maybe we should continue
the game with a few suggestions to get their attention and prevent at
least a few disasters."

Rat Traps

Life is cool.
Death sucks.
Don't get AIDS.

Living well is cool.
Being poor sucks.
Don't get married right away.

"Of course," said Dooley, "if they are going to be TINKs *[Two Incomes, No Kids, Beavis]*, the suggestion doesn't apply; the big risk is that they'll be NITKAPs *[No Income, Two Kids and Pets]*.

Don't get pregnant right away, it could ruin your whole life.

"You know," said Dooley, "money isn't everything, but saddle yourself with a couple of kids and animals, and money suddenly gets pretty high up on the daily discussion agenda."

Don't get convicted of a felony.

"The thing about this," said Dooley "is that it would keep them out of government jobs, and by the time they get ready to join the work force, government jobs may be all there are."

Dooley and I worked hard the next few days, adding options and choices, and by the time it was ready for testing, Rat Race seemed to take a growing interest in each player.

> **What's your name?**
> **Juanita-Maria**
> **What grade in school?**
> **Eleven**
> **Your grade average?**
> **A**
> **You wish. What is it really? I'm not going to tell anybody.**
> **B**
> **Hey, that's cool. How far are you going in school?**
> **High school**
> **What do you want to work at?**
> **Video game repair**
> **Stay in touch with Dooley. He understands. You could start at $300 a week. Withholding knocks $60 off that, so you take home $240.**

That's $1,080 a month. You should share rent with some friends and pay no more than $260 a month. That leaves you with $800 a month to live on. I'm going to take a wild guess at what you need in your life.

Car	$470

At this point Juanita-Maria hit the ? key and Rat Race explained

Payments $200, insurance $150, maintenance $40, gas and oil $80, total $470 a month. Trust me.

Car	$470
Telephone	50
Cable TV	25
Movies	20
CDs	20
Clothes	50
Rock concerts	20
Chow	225
Healthcare	20
Total	$900

Any chance of getting $100 a month from your parents?

Juanita-Maria hit "N."

How about doing without the car? Would you try living close to work
and walking, biking, and using public transportation? If you did,
you'd be golden; otherwise you're mega-bummed.

"Probably not," she typed.

Well, think about it, Juanita-Maria. You should cut $100 out of your
budget somewhere. Come back and play again soon. I'll keep
this talk in memory so you won't have to start all over. Good luck,
Juanita-Maria, and buckle up!

By the end of the first week, there was a long line of kids waiting to
play Rat Race.

Better to know where
important traps are before
starting your journey.

ROOFTOP RUMINATION – STRETCHWORK 10

Archibald, Crunch, and Dooley once did a consulting job for the Salk Institute in La Jolla.

The key players were all molecular biologists, several of them Nobel laureates.

Working on what they chose to work on, they seemed fulfilled and calm, yet somehow excited at the same time. They didn't care a fig for drapes, carpets, office furniture, decoration, or the trappings of power. They were almost completely unaware of the environmental limitations of the Institute.

One of them said, "We're driven by internal needles; no external stimuli seem important."

We would all be lucky to find work as satisfying.

Stretchwork 10

1. Something we're good at, getting better at, and enjoy doing.
2. The work makes us feel special.
3. It will help others if we succeed.
4. We have no excuses for not doing our best.
5. The trick is getting paid for it.

Note: There is evidence on another of Crunch's disks called "Letters I never got an answer to" that the Salk Institute experience led Crunch to see the need for small companies to keep track of the perceived enjoyability and meaningfulness of work if they were to retain their excitement, creativity, and energy. This, of course, led to the collaboration with Dooley on the invention of QuoVadoTron.

Jennifer Stepnowski
August 27, 2065

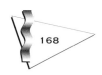

Preoccupation
with new lifestyles may preclude
finding right life's work.

COORDINATES:
   Kathleen Graciosa
   Accounting Dept
   Clerk
COMPANY: Droids R Us
CEO: Sterling Mentor
AGE: 45
**AVERAGE ENERGY
   LEVEL—COMPANY
   GOAL:** FW-3
QUERY: How am I
   spending my
   energy?

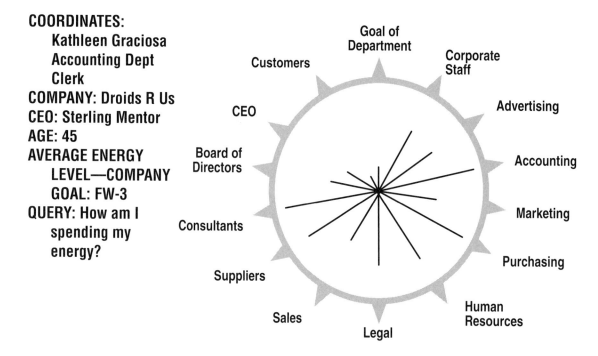

EVALUATION: Another success. Shortly after calling for this analysis of
herself, Ms. Graciosa had a talk with her boss and the two of them
worked out a more challenging role than checking purchasing
vouchers.

VIGNETTE: CONVERSATION OVERHEARD ON A SAN PEDRO STREET

EXT. COFFEE SHOP - DAY

TWO PEOPLE pause at the door of a coffee shop, then continue walking past.

> BOBBY
> I can't go in there.

> PATRICIA
> Why not?

> BOBBY
> Harry's in there.

> PATRICIA
> So?

> BOBBY
> He wants me back on time after lunch.

[CONTINUED]

                    PATRICIA
And?

                    BOBBY
I like to be late, and he doesn't
pay me enough to be back on
time.

Boss and worker both
lose when the work becomes Fetch:
good-bye, energy.

CELEBRATION

When the storefronts were ready to be turned over to the landlords, a huge daily royalty remittance arrived in my bank from QuoVadoTron. It was then that I had my epiphany.

I'd been assuming that the kids would disappear when school was over. But our regulars weren't going anywhere. They'd probably be spending even more time at the Test Center and taking aikido lessons.

After a hasty strategy conference with Archibald, Dooley, Lee, and Juanita-Maria, I negotiated five-year leases (with options to extend) on all of the storefronts.

When the new leases were signed we decided to have a celebration. Archibald flew in, and we all gathered in Dooley's kitchen: Lee, Archibald, Dooley, Juanita-Maria, Jeffrey, Bud, and Floyd were all there.

"Who'll we invite?" asked Dooley.

"How about a representative from each of the organizations that opposed us?" I suggested. I showed Dooley the latest of the weekly lists of enemies that Archibald was sending me.

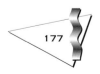

177

Opponents

Parents
Teachers
PTA
School Administrators
Local Politicians
Government Officials
Police
Medical Community
Press
Army
Navy
Marines
Air Force
Writers Guild of America
ASCAP

BMI
All Meat Associations
Cheese Industry
Processed Food Manufacturers
Tobacco Institute
Distilleries
Fast Food Franchises
Martial Arts Association
Mayor and City Council of San
    Pedro
Mayor and City Council of
    Moreno Valley
Pastors
Priests
Rabbis

"Well, that's too many people, and they wouldn't enjoy it anyway," said Dooley. "We'd have to jump around giving each other high-fives and we'd probably get jailed for showboating or taunting."

"So it's the eight of us," I said. "Who wants to name the poison?"

"Planet burgers and Snapple for me," said Juanita-Maria. The other kids, Lee, and Dooley went along with this.

"If you don't mind, Crunch and I will drink the best Cabernet Sauvignon," said Archibald. "As you know, that wine comes from the same grape that produces the famous claret or red Bordeaux in France.

"And there is a French legend that, once upon a time, there was a sickly baby who was sole heir to the Dukedom of Rochefoucauld. His parents despaired, but, unbeknownst to them, the baby's nurse was feeding him a spoonful of red bordeaux with every meal. The baby prospered, continued to consume red bordeaux in increasing amounts, and ultimately buried four wives and at least one mistress and died with a smile on his face at age 91.

"The reason we drink the best is that we don't drink much," Archibald continued. "I agree with Dooley's idea that two glasses a day is enough.

"Because alcohol is a mixed blessing. Or a mixed curse. And if I'm going to whack my liver and kidneys, I'm not going to whack 'em with Château La Foot Screwtop Special."

"Archibald," I said, "I think we can safely add the vineyards and the Wine-Grape Growers Association to our list of enemies."

"I'll have a glass of that," said Juanita-Maria.

"In your dreams," said Dooley. "You wouldn't like the taste, it would make you dizzy, and we'd all go to jail."

"There's a minor complication, beyond the issue of minors," announced Crunch. "We don't have any Cabernet, so Archibald and I will have planet burgers and Snapple, too."

Celebration marks
success. End of project or
at least end of week.

EXODUCTION

Well, I guess it's a beginning. We may not have saved the B² Generation, but we've given them a few skills and some useful ideas.

Some of the seeds we may have planted

Good role models: Dooley and Lee
Mediocre role model: Crunch
Acceptable use of power: Archibald
Tapping into the Federal trough
Connection between decent school grades and having fun
Connection between education and living well
Career/life choices
Having fun with words: creativity
An early career in the military for the disadvantaged
Straightforwardness and trust
Joint governance/shared responsibility
Plight of the poor and homeless

A taste of living well with less stuff
Value of skillful networking
Giving thought to our effect on the environment
Literature/music as a blessing in life
Connection between food, and exercise and feeling and looking good
Learning to enjoy cultural diversity
Elements of storytelling
Importance of playfulness
Connection between mind and body in the art of self-defense
Some rat traps in the rat race of life
Connection between work and play
Learning a few tenets of at least one major world religion

We were planning to reopen in September when school started (if you want to make God laugh, tell Her your plans), but even if we did, we wouldn't have known for several more years how we were doing.

A few people came in to see about buying a franchise. We told them to go ahead, it was free, but if they invented anything successful, to tell us about it via e-mail. Enough good ideas came in to warrant starting an e-mail newsletter.

"Can we make a difference?" I asked Dooley and Lee.

"Look at it this way," said Dooley. "Have you got anything better to do?"

Lee went down to start a class, and Dooley got that glazed look he gets whenever a beta version of a new CD-ROM is waiting on his desk to be checked out.

So I was left in geezerlike solitude, alone with my thoughts.

"You are what you eat," said Gaylord Hauser. ThunderBuns illustrated that. But we also are what we see and hear on TV, radio, and in movies. Of course, if you don't like what we are becoming, you can always try to play King Canute.

You could regulate the media. Add an "S" rating for Stupid. Try to control sex, violence, and bad language. Or you can have TV hours regulated like pub hours in Great Britain so there would be large parts of the day and night when people would have to rise from their couches and do something else or stay on their couches and stare at a blank tube. But censorship won't work in America and TV hours would be defeated by popping cassettes into VCRs (couching toward Bethlehem?).

Maybe it's the saner course to admit that man is God's funniest joke and that She built in a gene that will cause man to destroy himself and his environment one way or another.

Maybe it comes down to this: Find a cabin near a source of potable water and learn to grow food and live without fossil fuels. Learn how to read again and listen to Haydn on your solar-powered disc player.

Or maybe we should just keep watching Seinfeld, Home Improvement, and The Larry Sanders Show on the tube.

From where I sit in the land of sun, smog, drive-by shootings and falling IQs, it's difficult to see a lot of happy endings. But, as Dooley says, we're having fun, we don't seem to be breaking any laws or hurting anybody, so what's the problem?

Do you mean you thought
you could buy all the answers
in this little book?

JENNIFER'S AFTERWORD

CRUNCH'S mysterious death in August of 2017 was the subject of numerous videos and a live pay-per-view docudrama that fall. The "CRUNCH Presents Interactive Mystery Series" on CD-ROM is still a brisk seller. (At this printing, Raindrop Stone, granddaughter of filmmaker Oliver Stone, has announced a film project "that will finally tell the true story behind the Crunch conspiracy.")

JEFFREY TOURS, after a hitch in the Navy, attended Motorola University and invented the "Studio in a Drawer," which allows kids to produce two-hour feature films every afternoon, complete with music, soundtrack, and effects.

BUD SHRAKE, after a distinguished career writing Tex-Mex fiction, invented the P.G.A.'s successful "Yikey Tour" for professional golfers over 70, and in the year 2030 succeeded Deane Beman as Commissioner.

FLOYD TURNER, after winning a Pulitzer for his writing on "The New Rocky and Bullwinkle Show," married a spy and moved to the Rogue River in Oregon, where they lived happily ever after.

JUANITA-MARIA FRANCESCA graduated from the famous school of modern languages at San Pedro University with a Ph.D. in Modern Languages and master's degrees in Ancient Hawaiian and Cherokee. Unimpressed by her brief World Presidency, she married, had five children, and became a character actress beloved by the whole world.

DOOLEY STEPNOWSKI, *looking not a day older than 35 at age 82, became an international spokesmodel for the Pritikin Longevity Center.*

LEE NA PING *was last seen boarding a plane after announcing his intention to spend the rest of his days meditating in a Himalayan cave.*

ARCHIBALD PETRIE *went on to create Ghost Writer, the popular TV sitcom about the publishing industry. Seymour has kept his elevator in good repair.*

Jennifer Stepnowski
San Pedro, California
August 2065

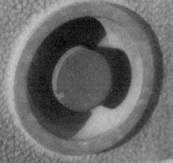